Coretta Scott King

History Maker Bios

Laura Hamilton Waxman

LERNER PUBLICATIONS COMPANY • MINNEAPOLIS

Lerner Publications Company
A division of Lerner Publishing Group, Inc.
241 First Avenue North
Minneapolis, MN 55401 U.S.A.

Website address: www.lernerbooks.com

Library of Congress Cataloging-in-Publication Data

Waxman, Laura Hamilton.
    Coretta Scott King / by Laura Hamilton Waxman.
      p.   cm. — (History maker biographies)
    Includes bibliographical references and index.
    ISBN 978-0-8225-7168-1 (lib. bdg. : alk. paper)
    1. King, Coretta Scott, 1927-2006—Juvenile literature. 2. African American
women civil rights workers—Biography—Juvenile literature. 3. Civil rights
workers—United States—Biography—Juvenile literature. 4. African
Americans—Biography—Juvenile literature. 5. King, Martin Luther, Jr.,
1929-1968—Juvenile literature. 6. African Americans—Civil rights—History—
20th century—Juvenile literature. 7. Civil rights movements—United States—
History—20th century—Juvenile literature. I. Title.
    E185.97.K47W39 2008
    323.092—dc22 [B]   2007017735

Manufactured in the United States of America
1 2 3 4 5 6 – JR – 13 12 11 10 09 08

TABLE OF CONTENTS

INTRODUCTION

Coretta Scott King grew up in the South in the 1930s. At the time, unfair laws kept black citizens from having basic rights. Coretta wanted to change those laws. She married a young preacher who had the same dream. His name was Martin Luther King Jr. Martin inspired other black Americans to stand up to unfair laws. So did Coretta. She gave speeches and concerts about the rights of black people.

In 1968, someone shot and killed Martin. Coretta could have led a quiet life after that. Instead, she shared Martin's ideas with people all over the world. She also spoke out against different kinds of unfair treatment. Coretta did all of this with strength, dignity, and pride.

This is her story.

1 GROWING UP PROUD

Coretta Scott was born on April 27, 1927, to a proud family. The Scotts lived on a small farm in west central Alabama. They grew corn, peas, and potatoes. They also raised hogs, cows, and chickens. The little wooden house they lived in had just two rooms, a kitchen and a bedroom. But it suited the family just fine.

Coretta tended the farm with her older sister, Edythe, and her younger brother, Obie. During cotton season, they earned money by picking cotton on white people's farms. Coretta worked for many hours underneath the burning sun. But she did not get tired. She was a strong and hard worker.

Obadiah Scott, Coretta's father, also worked hard. He earned money by moving logs in his truck from a white man's land to a nearby sawmill. On nights and weekends, Obadiah became the local barber. Black men would line up in front of his porch for haircuts.

Coretta, like this girl, worked in cotton fields as a child. Many black children in the 1930s earned money that way.

Coretta's parents taught her to strive for a better life. They taught her to have dignity and self-respect. They also taught her that she was as good as any white person.

In the 1930s, segregation kept black and white people apart. Unfair segregation laws treated black people as less important than white people. Coretta saw this most clearly in the nearby town of Marion. Black people could not stay in hotels or enter most restaurants there. To go into the drugstore, they had to use the side door. At the movie theater, they had to sit on hard wooden seats in the hot balcony.

To eat in this restaurant in the South, black and white customers had to use separate entrances.

Coretta and other black children in the area went to a different school than white children. One hundred black children squeezed into Coretta's one-room schoolhouse. The white children went to a large brick school with many classrooms.

Coretta had to walk three miles to school. Each day, a school bus carrying the white children passed her by. That made Coretta angry. But she didn't see how things would ever change.

Schools for black children often had old furniture and books.

Coretta's mother, Bernice, believed that education was the key to a better life. She encouraged her children to work hard in school. After Coretta finished sixth grade, she went to a private school for black students in Marion. It was called Lincoln High School.

At Lincoln High, Coretta fell in love with the world of music. She learned to read music and to play the trumpet and the piano. She took voice lessons and sang in the choir. She even became the director of her church's youth choir when she was about fifteen.

HOLDING HER HEAD HIGH

Lincoln High was one of the best schools for black children in the area. Both white and black teachers worked there. But some of the townspeople treated Lincoln's teachers and students cruelly. White teenagers called Coretta names. They tried to push the black students off the sidewalk. Coretta held her head high. She knew she was as good as anyone else.

While Coretta was in high school, her father bought two new trucks. They helped him start his own sawmill business. By that time, he had also moved his family into a six-room house. His success was rare in the African American community. And not everyone liked it.

Someone burned both the house and business to the ground. Coretta's family believed jealous white neighbors had started the fires. But Obadiah did not give up. He opened a grocery store and gas station instead.

Coretta admired her father's determination. But she had had enough of the South. She wanted to go to the North. Coretta had heard the North had no segregation. Black people were treated more fairly. Coretta was ready for a change.

2 LIFE UP NORTH

In 1945, eighteen-year-old Coretta graduated from high school at the top of her class. Her sister, Edythe, was already attending Antioch College in Ohio. Coretta decided to join her there. The school had just begun to accept black students. Coretta was one of three black students in a freshman class of more than three hundred.

Coretta loved her new school. She continued to study music and singing. She also studied to become a teacher.

For part of her studies, Coretta had to teach at a local school for a year. Both black and white students went to the school. But only white teachers taught there. The school refused to take Coretta as a teacher.

Coretta taught at a private school run by the college instead. However, she felt discouraged. She thought she had left segregation behind. But even in the North, she discovered, black people were not treated as equals.

A white music teacher teaches black and white students in the 1940s. In many cities in the North, only whites were allowed to teach white children.

Coretta was tired of waiting for things to change. She wanted to make a difference. She joined groups such as the National Association for the Advancement of Colored People (NAACP). Members of the NAACP worked to bring equality to black people.

THE NAACP

A small group of men and women formed the NAACP in 1909. They wanted to end segregation and other unfair treatment of black citizens. They challenged unfair laws in court. The NAACP also organized protests against segregation. Their work helped to end some of the worst segregation laws. The organization still works to make life better for black citizens all over the United States.

Coretta joined the NAACP while studying at Antioch College.

Coretta graduated from Antioch in 1951. At the age of twenty-four, she had big dreams. She wanted to become a professional singer. That meant more years of school to train her voice.

Coretta moved to Boston, Massachusetts. There she began studying at the New England Conservatory of Music.

Coretta's musical training kept her busy. But she also had some time for fun. One afternoon, she went on a date with a young man named Martin Luther King Jr. Martin had grown up in the South, like Coretta. He was getting an advanced degree in religion at Boston University. Then he planned to be a minister, just like his father.

Over lunch, Coretta and Martin talked about the world and how it could be better. They talked about the problems black people faced in the North and the South. They talked about the ways that poor people were treated unfairly.

Coretta admired Martin's quick mind and lively personality. He had a lot of charm and confidence. Coretta realized he was special. They continued to date and quickly fell in love.

Martin wanted to marry Coretta. But Coretta knew that most married women at the time did not have careers. If she married Martin, she would have to give up her dream of a singing career.

Coretta loved the idea of becoming a professional singer. But she realized that she loved Martin more. She married him on June 18, 1953. The wedding took place on her family's lawn in Alabama. Coretta was ready to begin a new life.

Martin and Coretta were happy young newlyweds.

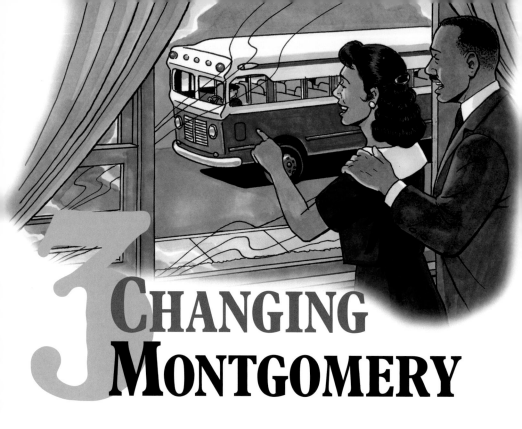

3 CHANGING MONTGOMERY

Coretta and Martin returned to Boston after the wedding to finish their studies. In 1954, Martin was offered a job in Montgomery, Alabama. He became a minister at the Dexter Avenue Baptist Church that fall.

Martin quickly made a name for himself in town. He became known as a powerful and uplifting preacher. The church members loved him and his quiet, dignified wife.

On November 17, 1955, the Kings had their first child. They named her Yolanda, or Yoki for short. Two weeks later, their lives changed forever.

On December 1, a black woman named Rosa Parks was arrested in Montgomery. She had broken a city segregation law. The law said that black people had to sit in the back of city buses. Only white people could sit in the front. And black passengers had to give up their seats to white people if the bus was full. Rosa had refused to give up her seat.

Black riders stand on a segregated bus in Alabama. Several seats are open in the white section.

Rosa Parks was taken to jail. An officer took her fingerprints there.

What happened to Rosa Parks angered black people. It upset Coretta and Martin too. They wanted to show the bus company that they wouldn't put up with such unfair rules anymore. Some black leaders decided to organize a bus boycott. They wanted the black citizens of Montgomery to stay off the buses for one day. Then the bus company would lose the money it usually earned from those riders' fares.

The group needed a leader to convince people to take part in the protest. They called on the powerful preacher Martin Luther King Jr.

Fighting School Segregation

The NAACP and other black citizens wanted to end segregation in schools. The NAACP took its case to the U.S. Supreme Court. All states must follow that court's decisions. The NAACP argued that segregation in schools was unfair. The Supreme Court agreed. In 1954, it outlawed segregation in schools. This case, *Brown v. Board of Education*, became an important turning point. It gave black people the courage to fight other segregation laws.

Coretta knew that many white people wanted the bus laws to stay the same. If Martin led the boycott, they would hate him. But Coretta believed in standing up for black people's rights. She did not hold Martin back. She hoped the boycott would be a success.

Martin gave powerful speeches. They helped inspire Montgomery's black citizens to keep up the boycott.

Coretta woke up early on the morning of the boycott. She looked out the front window of their house. From there, she could see a nearby bus stop. Soon a bus arrived. Coretta shouted for Martin to come quickly. The bus was empty!

Many city buses were empty that day. The boycott was more successful than anyone had imagined it could be. Martin and other leaders encouraged the black community to continue the protest. They would stay off the buses until the bus company agreed to treat them more fairly.

People across the country admired Martin for his leadership. But many of Montgomery's white people did not. Coretta received angry phone calls. The callers threatened to hurt her husband and her family. Coretta stayed calm. She would not let those people scare her.

One night in January 1956, Martin was away giving a speech. Coretta stayed at home caring for Yoki. Suddenly, she heard a loud thud on the front porch. As she ran to the back of the house, a bomb went off on the porch. Windows shattered and smoke filled the rooms. Coretta and Yoki escaped without getting hurt.

After the bomb went off, an angry crowd of black people came to the King home. Martin (RIGHT) calmed them down.

Martin rushed home when he heard the news. Coretta's father came to take Coretta and Yoki home to his farm. He thought they would be safer there. But Coretta would not go. She planned to stay by her husband's side no matter what.

In November 1956, the U.S. Supreme Court said that segregation on buses was against U.S. law. Segregation on the Montgomery buses ended. So did the bus boycott. Martin and Coretta were thrilled. But they knew many more unfair laws still had to change.

Coretta and Martin (FRONT, FIFTH AND FOURTH FROM LEFT) wait for a bus together after the boycott ended.

4 STAYING STRONG

After the bus boycott, black people in other cities began to speak out against unfair treatment. They took part in what became known as the civil rights movement. Members of this movement fought for the right of all black citizens to be treated fairly and equally. Martin became the movement's most famous leader. He gave speeches all over the country.

Martin's work kept him away from home a lot. Coretta was always glad to see him on his return.

Coretta missed Martin when he was away. But she didn't complain. She believed in her husband and his ideas.

Martin knew that many white people didn't want African Americans to gain more rights. He knew those whites would try to hurt black people in the movement. But he did not think black people should fight back with violence. Instead, he said they should stand up for themselves peacefully. He believed peaceful protest was the only way to make lasting changes.

Martin's work often put him in danger. Angry white citizens continued to threaten him and his family. Police often arrested him for protesting and put him in jail. Through it all, Coretta stayed calm and positive. Her strength kept Martin strong during the hardest times.

In 1960, the Kings moved to Martin's hometown of Atlanta, Georgia. From there, Martin traveled all over the South leading the civil rights movement.

Coretta and Martin watch Marty (born in 1957) and Yoki play catch in their Atlanta home in 1960.

WORKING FOR PEACE

In 1962, Coretta traveled to Geneva, Switzerland, with forty-nine other women. They belonged to the Women's International League for Peace and Freedom. In Geneva, they met with U.S. and Russian leaders. They asked for those countries to stop testing nuclear bombs, which are made for wars. The women believed that war was wrong. They also worried that the tests caused health problems for people living nearby.

Coretta spent most of her time caring for her family. By 1963, she and Martin had three more children. They were named Martin, Dexter, and Bernice. Still, Coretta found time to give speeches about the civil rights movement. Like Martin, she spoke out against violence.

On August 28, 1963, Coretta joined Martin in the March on Washington. At this protest, 250,000 people filled the streets of Washington, D.C., the U.S. capital. They marched to demand equal rights for black citizens. The protest showed that black people were serious about wanting change.

Back home, Coretta began to organize what she called Freedom Concerts. The first one took place in New York City in 1964. In these concerts, she sang and read poetry. She spoke out against unfair treatment of black people. Famous musicians also performed. Money from the ticket sales went to help the civil rights movement.

(FROM LEFT TO RIGHT) Yoki, Bernice, Dexter, and Marty practiced singing freedom songs with Coretta.

*President Lyndon B. Johnson (SEATED) signs the Civil
Rights Act of 1964. Martin stands behind the president.*

That same year, Coretta and Martin
celebrated a victory for African Americans.
President Lyndon Johnson signed the Civil
Rights Act of 1964. This law made
segregation illegal in hotels, restaurants,
and other places. Businesses could not hire
a white person instead of a black person
simply because of skin color. Schools and
colleges could not keep out black students.

But southern states still kept black people from voting. They used unfair fees and tests to turn away black voters. So black people could not help to choose fair leaders.

In March 1965, Martin led a large protest against unfair voting laws. Marchers walked from Selma, Alabama, to the state's capitol in Montgomery. Coretta was proud to march alongside her husband. They hoped the protest would help bring change.

Their wish came true when President Johnson signed a new law. The Voting Rights Act of 1965 said that no state could stand in the way of a citizen's right to vote.

On March 21, 1965, Coretta and Martin led more than three thousand marchers out of Selma, Alabama. Thousands of others joined them along the way to Montgomery.

Martin had become a hero to many people. But many others hated him for his beliefs. Coretta knew that people still wanted to hurt or kill him. She lived with that fear every day. But she never stopped believing in her husband.

In April 1968, Martin traveled to Memphis, Tennessee, to help lead a protest. On April 4, Coretta received some terrible news. Someone had shot Martin. He died a little while later. That day, Coretta felt that a part of her had died too. But she knew she had to be strong for her children.

Yoki, Marty, Martin's brother, A.D., Coretta, and Bernice at Martin's funeral

Yoki asked Coretta a question all the King children wondered about. She wanted to know if she should hate the man who killed their father. Coretta told her daughter not to hate anyone, not even that man.

Coretta believed that hatred only made problems worse. Instead of feeling hatred, she told her children to feel proud. Their father had risked his life to help others. Coretta was proud of him too.

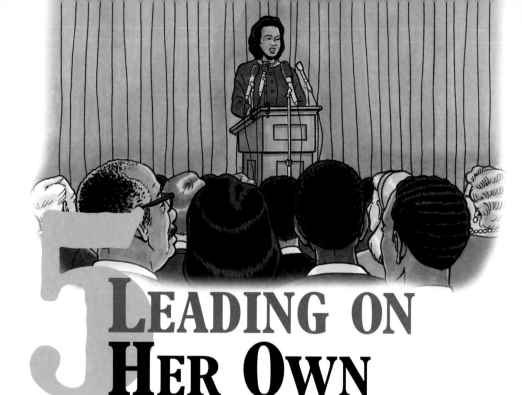

5 LEADING ON HER OWN

Coretta missed Martin terribly. She knew she could not bring him back. But she could work to keep his memory and dreams alive.

Coretta went to Martin's funeral five days after he died. She felt deep sadness about his death. But, as always, she stayed calm and strong. She hoped everyone who missed Martin would stay strong too. That way, they could keep working for change.

Without Martin, Coretta had to take care of her family on her own. But she still found time to go to protests and give speeches. In June, she went to a large gathering in Washington, D.C. It was part of the Poor People's Campaign. Martin had started this movement before he died. He had wanted to improve housing, education, and wages for poor people of all races.

Protesters in the Poor People's Campaign arrived in Washington, D.C., on May 12, 1968. Thousands lived in tents on the Washington Mall for about one month.

Coretta spoke to thousands of people at the 1968 Poor People's Campaign rally in Washington, D.C.

At the event in Washington, Coretta spoke in front of thousands of people. She knew that most of the other speakers were men. Not many women had been leaders in the civil rights movement. She wanted to help change that.

Coretta spoke about Martin's dreams for a better world. Then she asked the women of the United States for their help. She asked them to help solve the problems of the nation's poor. She also asked them to help end war and the unfair treatment of people of color. She knew they could make a big difference if they worked together.

That same month, Coretta began working on a dream of her own. She wanted to honor her husband by opening the Martin Luther King Jr. Center for Nonviolent Social Change. She planned to use the King Center to teach Martin's ideas to others.

Coretta needed to raise a lot of money to build the King Center. She began traveling all over the country and the world. She shared Martin's ideas with people. She also asked people to help pay for a building to honor his work and memory.

Coretta gave talks about Martin's ideas. She asked people to help pay for the Martin Luther King Jr. Center.

At the same time, Coretta went to many more protests in Martin's honor. She also fought for women to be treated equally to men. She spoke out for peace and ending war. And she worked to help poor people find good jobs with fair pay.

By 1981, Coretta had helped to raise millions of dollars for the new King Center. It opened that year in Atlanta. Coretta led the center as its president.

THE CORETTA SCOTT KING BOOK AWARD

A year after Martin died, two librarians created the Coretta Scott King Book Award. It honors books for young people written by black authors. In 1970, the first book to win the award was *Martin Luther King Jr.: Man of Peace* by Lillie Patterson. A new book has received the award each year. The award also honors an outstanding black illustrator each year.

Visitors to the King Center see the Martin Luther King Jr. tomb. It is surrounded by a reflecting pool in front of Freedom Hall.

The King Center includes a museum about Martin and the civil rights movement. It also has a library, an auditorium, and rooms for meetings and lectures. Up to one million people visit the King Center each year.

Coretta was proud of the King Center. But she had another big dream. She wanted to create a national holiday in Martin's memory. Coretta worked with U.S. leaders to make her dream come true.

In 1983, President Ronald Reagan signed a bill into law. It said that the country would celebrate Martin Luther King Jr. Day each year. Coretta happily celebrated the first Martin Luther King Jr. holiday on January 20, 1986.

Coretta (FRONT LEFT) watches President Reagan (SEATED) sign a bill. The bill created the Martin Luther King Jr. holiday.

During the 1980s and 1990s, Coretta continued to work for the fair treatment of others. She especially fought for the rights of black citizens in the country of South Africa. They lived under cruel apartheid laws. Apartheid was like segregation. It kept apart black people and white people. Apartheid took away the rights of black South Africans. Coretta and many others spoke out against apartheid. It finally ended in the early 1990s.

Nelson Mandela helped end apartheid. He was elected president of South Africa in 1994. Coretta celebrated with him when he won the election.

By the 2000s, Coretta was in her
seventies. She no longer ran the King
Center. But she never stopped working
for a nonviolent world. In 2003, as the
United States prepared to go to war with
the country of Iraq, Coretta spoke out. She
still felt that all wars were wrong. She
believed fighting was not the best way to
solve problems.

In 2003, Coretta
(CENTER) attended
the dedication of
a plaque honoring
Martin's "I have a
dream" speech.
The plaque
(BOTTOM) is on
the steps of the
Lincoln Memorial.
Martin gave this
famous speech
there in 1963.

In her last years, Coretta tried to lead a quieter life. She continued to speak out when she had something important to say. But she spent more time at home with her family and friends.

Coretta died on January 30, 2006. More than ten thousand people came to her funeral. They remembered the many ways she kept her husband's dream alive. And they admired her for helping to make life fairer and more peaceful for all.

TIMELINE

In the year . . .

1945   Coretta began attending Antioch College.   Age 18

1951   she graduated from Antioch and started attending the New England Conservatory.

1953   she married Martin Luther King Jr. on June 18.   Age 26

1955   her first child, Yolanda (Yoki), was born on November 17.
the Montgomery bus boycott began.

1956   the Supreme Court outlawed segregation of Montgomery's buses in November, and the bus boycott ended.

1957   Coretta's son Martin was born on October 23.   Age 30

1961   her son Dexter was born on January 30.

1962   she traveled to Geneva, Switzerland, to protest the testing of nuclear bombs.

1963   her daughter Bernice was born on March 28.

1964   Coretta began performing Freedom Concerts.   Age 37

1968   Martin Luther King Jr. was killed on April 4.
she attended a protest for the Poor People's Campaign in Washington, D.C., in June.

1981   the Martin Luther King Jr. Center for Nonviolent Social Change opened.   Age 54

1983   President Ronald Reagan signed a law creating Martin Luther King Jr. Day.

2003   she spoke out against going to war with Iraq.

2006   she died on January 30.   Age 78

A SPECIAL PLACE

Coretta chose a special spot for the King Center. It is located in Atlanta, Georgia, in Martin's old neighborhood. Part of the neighborhood has become the Martin Luther King Jr. National Historic Site. It is open to visitors who want to tour the place where he grew up.

Just one block away from the King Center sits Martin's childhood home. Inside, visitors can see the kind of furniture, wallpaper, and dishes that Martin's family had when they lived in the house.

Across from the King Center is Ebenezer Baptist Church. Martin's father led this church for many years. Later, Martin helped lead it when he and Coretta moved to Atlanta.

A tomb lies outside the center. This monument marks the place where Coretta and Martin are buried. In front of the tomb is the Eternal Flame. It burns day and night, all year long. The flame helps remind visitors to keep Martin and Coretta's dreams alive.

A visitor to the King Center photographs a mural of Coretta.

45

FURTHER READING

NONFICTION

Landau, Elaine. *The Civil Rights Movement in America.* **New York: Children's Press, 2003.** This book describes the history of the U.S. civil rights movement.

Miller, Jake. *The March from Selma to Montgomery: African Americans Demand the Vote.* **New York: PowerKids Press, 2004.** This book tells the story of the famous protest that helped end unfair voting laws for African Americans.

Shore, Diane Z., and Jessica Alexander. *This Is the Dream.* **New York: HarperCollins Publishers, 2006.** This title combines poetry, photographs, and illustrations to tell the story of the civil rights movement.

Winget, Mary. *Martin Luther King Jr.* **Minneapolis: Lerner Publications Company, 2003.** This biography talks about the famous civil rights leader.

FICTION

Armistead, John. *The $66 Summer.* **Minneapolis: Milkweed Editions, 2000.** Thirteen-year-old George faces the painful truth of segregation in Alabama in the 1950s.

Weatherford, Carole Boston. *Freedom on the Menu: The Greensboro Sit-Ins.* **New York: Dial, 2004.** This picture book tells the story of the fight to end segregation in the South from the point of view of a girl in 1960.

WEBSITES

Coretta Scott King Interview
http://www.achievement.org/autodoc/page/kin1int-1 This website features an interesting interview with Coretta about her life and her beliefs.

The King Center Official Website
http://www.thekingcenter.org Visit this website to learn more about the center that Coretta created in memory of her husband.

Martin Luther King Jr. Day on the Net
http://www.holidays.net/mlk Learn about the holiday that honors Coretta's husband.

SELECT BIBLIOGRAPHY

Applebome, Peter. "Coretta Scott King, 78, Widow of Dr. Martin Luther King Jr., Dies." *New York Times*, January 31, 2006, A1.

Estate of Martin Luther King, Jr. "Papers of Martin Luther King, Jr.: Coretta Scott King." *Stanford University.* n.d. http://www.stanford.edu/group/King/about_king/details/270427b.htm (June 20, 2007).

King, Coretta Scott. *My Life with Martin Luther King, Jr.* New York: Henry Holt and Company, 1993.

King, Dexter Scott, and Ralph Wiley. *Growing up King: An Intimate Memoir.* New York: Intellectual Properties Management/Warner Books, 2003.

King, Martin Luther, Jr. *The Autobiography of Martin Luther King, Jr.* Clayborne Carson, ed. New York: Intellectual Properties Management, Inc./Warner Books, 1998.

INDEX

Photo Acknowledgments

The images in this book are used with the permission of: © Jim Smeal/WireImage/Getty Images, p. 4; © Dorothea Lang/Stringer/Time & Life Pictures/Getty Images, p. 7; Library of Congress, pp. 8, 19; © Gordon Parks/Time & Life Pictures/Getty Images, p. 9; *St. Paul Dispatch & Pioneer Press*/Minnesota Historical Society, p. 13; © The Everett Collection, p. 15; © Michael Ochs Archives/CORBIS, p. 16; © Bettmann/CORBIS, pp. 17, 23, 29, 35; © AP Photo/Gene Herrick, pp. 20, 22, 26; © Don Cravens/Time & Life Pictures/Getty Images, p. 24; © Donald Uhrbrock/Time & Life Pictures/Getty Images, p. 27; The Lyndon B. Johnson Presidential Library, p. 30; © AP Photo/File, p. 31; © Hulton Archive/Getty Images, pp. 32, 36; © Michael Ochs Archives/Stringer/Getty Images, p. 37; © AP Photo/Ric Feld, p. 39; National Archives, p. 40; © David Turnley/CORBIS, p. 41; © Mannie Garcia/ZUMA Press, p. 42; © AP Photo/John Bazemore, p. 45.

Front cover: © Vernon Merritt III/Time & Life Pictures/Getty Images
Back cover: © Bettmann/CORBIS